13 .

Cleopatra

Jane Bingham

Heinemann
LIBRARY

www.heinemann.co.uk/library
Visit our website to find out more information about **Heinemann** books.

To order:
☎ Phone 44 (0) 1865 888112
🖷 Send a fax to 44 (0) 1865 314091
🖥 Visit the Heinemann Bookshop at **www.heinemann.co.uk/library** to browse our catalogue and order online.

Heinemann Library is an imprint of **Pearson Education Limited**, a company incorporated in England and Wales having its registered office at Edinburgh Gate, Harlow, Essex, CM20 2JE – Registered company number: 00872828 Heinemann is a registered trademark of Pearson Education Limited.

Text © Pearson Education Limited 2009
First published in hardback in 2009
The moral rights of the proprietor have been asserted.

Edited by Louise Galpine and Catherine Clarke
Designed by Kimberly R. Miracle, Jennifer Lacki and Betsy Wernert
Original illustrations © Pearson Education Limited
Illustrations by Mapping Specialists
Picture research by Hannah Taylor
Originated by Modern Age
Printed in China by Leo Paper Group

ISBN 978 0 431044 73 6 (hardback)
13 12 11 10 09
10 9 8 7 6 5 4 3 2

British Library Cataloguing in Publication Data
Bingham, Jane
Cleopatra. – (Levelled Biographies)
932'.021'092
A full catalogue record for this book is available from the British Library.

Acknowledgements
We would like to thank the following for permission to reproduce photographs:
©akg-images p. **15**; ©Alamy (ClassicStock) p. **13**; ©Ancient Art & Architecture Collection (Mary Jelliffe) p. **6**; ©The Art Archive pp. **7**, **11** (Egyptian Museum Cairo/Dagli Orti), **14** (Galleria d'Arte Moderna Rome/Dagli Orti), **16** (Bibliotheque Musee du Louvre/Gianni Dagli Orti); ©The Bridgeman Art Library pp. **8** (Edfu, Province of Aswan, Egypt), **17** (Private Collection), **19** (Peterhof Palace, Petrodvorets, St Petersburg, Russia), **21** (Temple of Hathor, Denderah, Egypt), **22** (Neue Galerie, Kassel, Germany/Museumslandschaft hessen Kassel/Ute Brunzel), **23** (Galleria Palazzo Corsini, Florence, Italy), **24** (Giraudon/Villa Barbarigo, Noventa Vicentina, Italy); ©Corbis pp. **4** (Bettmann), **9** (Sandro Vannini), **25** (Bettmann), **27** (Bettmann); ©Getty Images (Time Life Pictures/Walter Sanders) p. **12**.

Cover photograph of a portrait of Cleopatra reproduced with permission of ©akg-images.

We would like to thank Nancy Harris for her invaluable help in the preparation of this book.

Every effort has been made to contact copyright holders of material reproduced in this book. Any omissions will be rectified in subsequent printings if notice is given to the publishers.

CONTENTS

Some words are shown in bold, **like this**. You can find out what they mean by looking in the glossary.

CLEOPATRA, QUEEN OF EGYPT

Cleopatra was queen of Egypt more than 2,000 years ago. She was very lively and clever. Her life was full of adventures. Two great leaders fell in love with her.

Egypt in danger

Cleopatra ruled the kingdom of Egypt for 21 years from 51 BCE to 30 BCE. At that time, Egypt was a wealthy country. It was a great centre for **trade** (buying and selling things). But some very powerful people had plans to **conquer** (take over) Egypt. These people were known as the **Romans**.

It is impossible for us to know what Queen Cleopatra really looked like, but this is one artist's idea.

Saving Egypt

Queen Cleopatra had a very important job. She had to keep her country safe from the Romans. While she was queen, she did her best to save Egypt.

How do we know?

After Cleopatra's death, some Roman writers told her story. But Cleopatra was their enemy. They did not write about her in a kind way. They said she was a wicked woman, who played tricks on the Romans. Today, nobody knows whether this was really true.

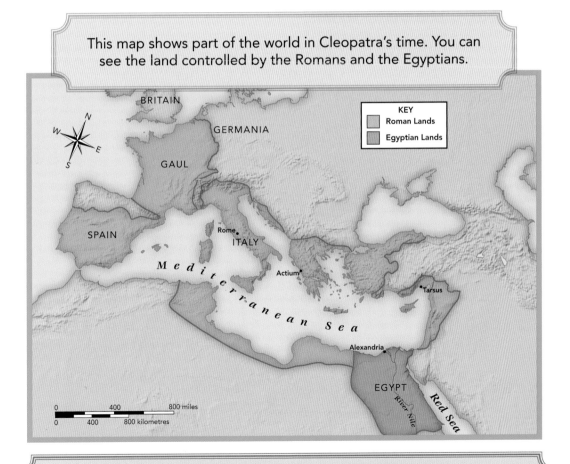

This map shows part of the world in Cleopatra's time. You can see the land controlled by the Romans and the Egyptians.

KEY
Roman Lands
Egyptian Lands

BRITAIN

GERMANIA

GAUL

SPAIN

Rome
ITALY

Actium

Tarsus

M e d i t e r r a n e a n   S e a

Alexandria

EGYPT

River Nile

Red Sea

0   400   800 miles
0   400   800 kilometres

BCE The letters BCE are used for all the dates before the Christian religion began. BCE dates are always counted backwards.

AN EGYPTIAN PRINCESS

Princess Cleopatra was born in the year 69 BCE. That was more than 2,000 years ago. She was the third daughter of the king and queen of Egypt. Her family had ruled Egypt for almost 300 years.

Life in the palace

Cleopatra grew up in a beautiful palace, in the city of Alexandria. The palace was built from a stone called **marble**. It had many rooms.

Cleopatra had three sisters and two brothers. All the royal children had lessons at the palace. A teacher showed them how to read and write.

This stone carving shows Egyptian children learning to write.

Toys and games

When they were young, the royal children played with dolls and model animals. As they grew older, they had **board games**. Playing board games taught Cleopatra to think clearly and plan ahead.

Ancient pyramids

The ancient kingdom of Egypt had many huge stone **pyramids**. Pyramids are tombs where kings are buried. The pyramids reminded Egyptians of their past. The pyramids were built along the banks of the River Nile.

This photograph shows the **sphinx** (left) and a pyramid. These were built 2,000 years before Cleopatra was born.

Jealous sisters

As a young girl, Cleopatra was clever and brave. This made her older sisters very jealous. They were afraid that their father would choose Cleopatra to be the next queen, instead of them.

One of her sisters was so jealous that she decided to poison her little sister. But Cleopatra heard about this plan just in time.

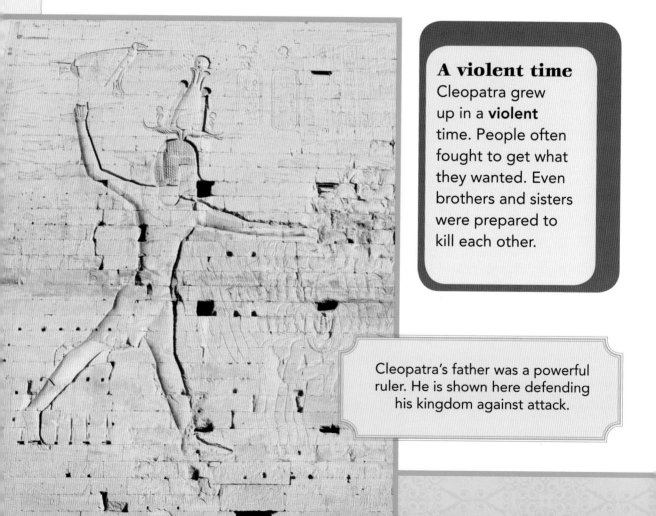

A violent time
Cleopatra grew up in a **violent** time. People often fought to get what they wanted. Even brothers and sisters were prepared to kill each other.

Cleopatra's father was a powerful ruler. He is shown here defending his kingdom against attack.

This Roman sculpture shows what Cleopatra might have looked like when she was young.

Keeping safe

Cleopatra ordered one of her servants to be her food-taster. The servant had to taste every dish that was served to Cleopatra. Before she began to eat, Cleopatra waited to check that the servant had not been poisoned.

Early lessons

Cleopatra never forgot her sisters' jealousy. At an early age, she learnt to look after herself. She also learnt to watch out for enemies everywhere.

Ruling Egypt

By 53 BCE Cleopatra was 16 years old. Both her older sisters were dead. They had tried to take power from their father. But they had both been killed. Now Cleopatra was the oldest daughter. When her father died, she would be queen, and her younger brother would be king.

Sharing the throne

Cleopatra's father died in 51 BCE when she was 18 years old. Straightaway, she was married to her 10-year-old brother, Ptolemy (say *TAH-le-mee*). In ancient Egypt, royal sisters and brothers often married. This meant all the power was kept in one family.

Starting to rule

Cleopatra and Ptolemy began to rule jointly in 51 BCE. But they often argued. Cleopatra wanted to rule alone. She had great plans to make Egypt more powerful.

Tutankhamen: the boy king

It was quite common to have very young rulers in ancient Egypt. A thousand years before Cleopatra's time, Egypt was ruled by a boy. His name was Tutankhamen. He was around eight or nine years old when he became king.

This is Tutankhamen's famous funeral mask.

CAESAR AND CLEOPATRA

Cleopatra and Ptolemy had many arguments. They both thought that they should rule alone. In 48 BCE Julius Caesar arrived in Egypt. He was the leader of the **Roman** army. He had plans to take over Egypt.

Caesar was determined to put an end to the arguments in Egypt. He said he would decide who should rule. Cleopatra and her brother agreed.

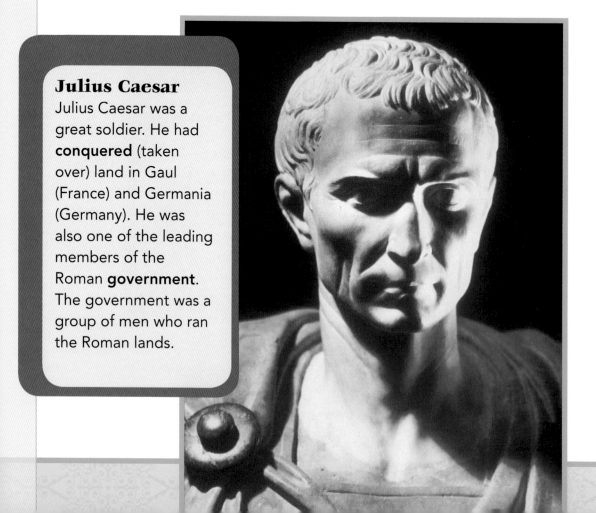

Julius Caesar
Julius Caesar was a great soldier. He had **conquered** (taken over) land in Gaul (France) and Germania (Germany). He was also one of the leading members of the Roman **government**. The government was a group of men who ran the Roman lands.

This is an artist's idea of Caesar's first meeting with Cleopatra. At the time they met, Caesar was 52 years old. Cleopatra was 21 years old.

A surprise meeting

Cleopatra wanted to meet Caesar and show him that she should rule. But he was staying in the palace with her brother. So she thought up a clever way to meet him. She arranged for a carpet to be presented to Caesar as a gift. Then she hid herself inside the rolled-up carpet.

When the carpet was unrolled, Caesar was amazed to see Cleopatra tumbling out of it. Over the next few days, he found out that she was very clever. It was not long before Caesar fell in love with Cleopatra.

A romantic journey

Caesar decided not to return to Rome. Instead he stayed in Egypt with Cleopatra. They sailed down the River Nile in a beautiful boat. Caesar and Cleopatra were very happy together. Soon Cleopatra was expecting a child.

A son is born

Cleopatra returned to Alexandria in 47 BCE, and gave birth to a son. He was called Caesarion, which means "little Caesar". Cleopatra dreamt that one day Caesarion would rule Egypt and Rome. But her dreams were soon shattered.

Caesar dies

While Caesar was in Egypt, he decided that he wanted to be king of Rome. When he went back to Rome, he took more power for himself. Many Romans feared that Caesar was growing too powerful.

This is an artist's idea of the murder of Julius Caesar.

Even Caesar's friends saw him as a danger. They decided he must die. In 44 BCE, Julius Caesar was stabbed to death. Now Cleopatra and her son were alone.

Caesar's will

Cleopatra hoped that Caesarion would **inherit** his father's wealth. But Caesar had left everything to his great-nephew, Octavian. Later, Octavian became a powerful enemy of Egypt.

Octavian later took the name of Augustus. He became the first Roman **Emperor** (leader).

ANTONY AND CLEOPATRA

After Caesar's death, there was **chaos** in Rome. Then, in 43 BCE two men took control. The two men were Octavian and Antony. Octavian ruled in the west. Antony ruled Rome's eastern lands. Antony was a brave and handsome leader in the **Roman** army.

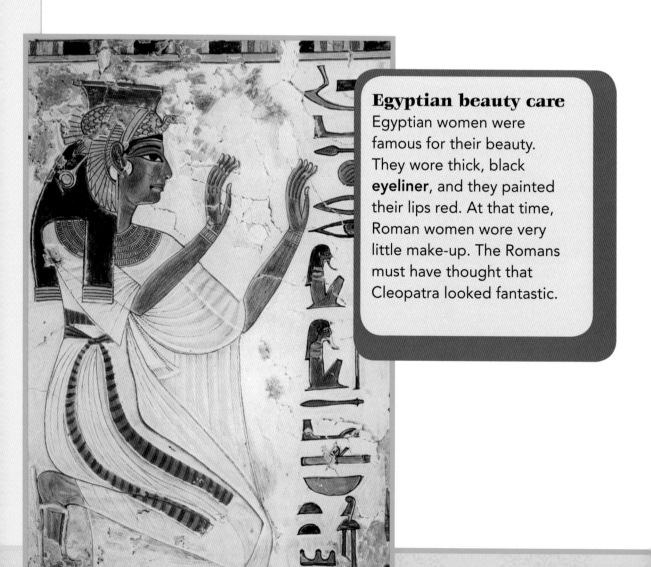

Egyptian beauty care
Egyptian women were famous for their beauty. They wore thick, black **eyeliner**, and they painted their lips red. At that time, Roman women wore very little make-up. The Romans must have thought that Cleopatra looked fantastic.

Antony's orders

Antony's lands were close to Egypt. He needed to be sure that the queen of Egypt would support him. He sent a messenger with orders for Cleopatra. She should sail to meet him at the **port** (harbour) of Tarsus.

Cleopatra hated to be given orders. So she decided to take her time. She wanted to show Antony that the queen of Egypt should be treated with **respect**.

Cleopatra arrives

Cleopatra's barge arrived in Tarsus in 41 BCE. It had huge purple sails. It was covered in silver and gold. But the finest sight of all was Queen Cleopatra, dressed in her royal robes. Antony was amazed.

This painting shows what Cleopatra might have looked like when her barge arrived at Tarsus.

Falling in love

Antony soon fell in love with the Egyptian queen. Cleopatra loved Antony too. They **respected** each other as leaders. They also had a lot of fun together.

Life in the palace

Antony and Cleopatra were very happy together. They lived a life of **luxury** (great comfort) in the royal palace at Alexandria. They also travelled a lot around Egypt. This meant Cleopatra could visit all her people. Even though Antony was often away at war, he returned to Egypt whenever he could.

Keeping Egypt safe

Cleopatra loved living with Antony. But she also had other reasons for staying with him. Antony was a great soldier, who ruled an enormous army. He could fight against Egypt's enemies.

Fun on the Nile

Antony and Cleopatra often went fishing on the River Nile. But Antony was not good at fishing. A famous story is told about a trick that Cleopatra played on Antony. One day, Cleopatra told a servant to dive into the water. He was to attach an old, dry fish to Antony's line. When Antony pulled up the fish, Cleopatra joked that he should hunt kingdoms rather than fish.

This painting shows Antony and Cleopatra side by side with servants all around them. The artist has painted Cleopatra with blonde hair.

A royal family

Antony and Cleopatra had three children. The oldest were twins: a boy and a girl. The youngest was a boy. Antony also acted as a father to Cleopatra's oldest son, Caesarion.

Land for the family

In 34 BCE, Antony decided to give his family some very special gifts. He held a grand **ceremony** in the royal palace. In this ceremony, he gave large areas of Roman land to Cleopatra and her four children.

This map shows the lands that Antony gave to Cleopatra and her children. It also shows the lands ruled by Octavian.

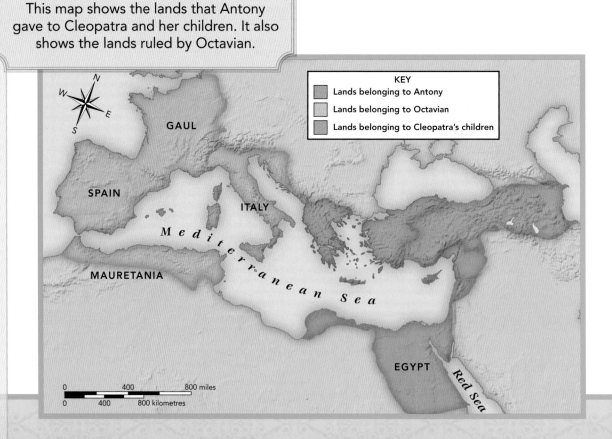

KEY

Lands belonging to Antony

Lands belonging to Octavian

Lands belonging to Cleopatra's children

Dangerous gifts

Antony's gifts made Cleopatra very happy. She dreamt that her children would rule over a huge **empire**. But not everyone was pleased about these gifts. It wasn't long before the news spread to Rome.

This stone carving from Egypt shows Cleopatra with her son Caesarion.

Land for Egypt
Most of the lands that Antony gave to Cleopatra and her children had once belonged to Egypt. But they had been **conquered** by Rome. Cleopatra was delighted to gain control of these lands. She felt that she had won back the ancient Egyptian lands.

War with Rome

Antony and Cleopatra became enemies of the Romans.

When they heard the news, the **Romans** were furious. They could not believe that Antony had given away Roman lands. Octavian was delighted that the people were unhappy with Antony. He wanted to rule Rome on his own.

Rumours and war

Octavian began to spread **rumours** that Cleopatra was a **sorceress**. He said she had cast an evil spell on Antony. Soon Octavian had turned all the Romans against Cleopatra. He declared war on Cleopatra in 31 BCE.

Antony and Cleopatra prepared for battle. They were ready to fight the Romans on land or sea.

The Battle of Actium

Octavian's **navy** trapped Antony's ships in the **port** of Actium. Antony waited many months, but finally he sailed out to fight. Antony and Cleopatra each led their own **fleet** (group) of ships.

Fighting at sea

In Cleopatra's time, countries often fought battles at sea. Both sides had long battle ships. Each ship had a long, pointed **prow** (the sharp end at the front of a boat). Leaders tried to hit an enemy ship with their boat's prow. This could make the other ship sink.

During battle, soldiers fired flaming arrows at their enemies. The arrows made the enemy ships catch fire.

This is one artist's idea of what the battle of Actium looked like.

Sailing away

Both sides fought bravely at Actium, but slowly Antony began to lose. Then Cleopatra did a very surprising thing. She turned her ships around and headed back to Egypt. When Antony saw Cleopatra sailing away, he raced after her as fast as he could.

A terrible defeat

Once it had lost its leader, Antony's **fleet** was easily defeated. Later, Octavian fought Antony in Egypt. Octavian won a second victory. The Romans had **conquered** the kingdom of Egypt.

Antony's despair

After Alexandria was conquered, Antony was filled with **despair**. Then he heard a **rumour** that Cleopatra was dead. He felt that he had lost everything. He wanted to die. So he stabbed himself.

As Antony lay dying, a messenger brought news. He said that Cleopatra was not dead after all. Antony was carried to Cleopatra, and died in her arms. It was 30 BCE.

What happened at Actium?

Nobody knows why Cleopatra sailed away from Actium. Her enemies said that she was a **coward**. Other people think she knew the battle was lost. They say she was returning home to strengthen her army.

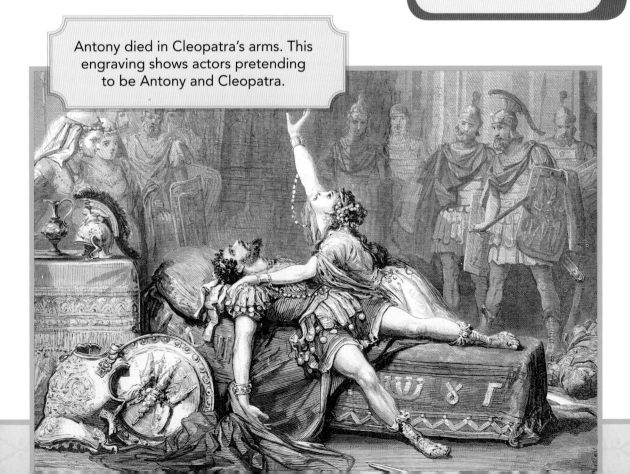

Antony died in Cleopatra's arms. This engraving shows actors pretending to be Antony and Cleopatra.

DEATH OF A QUEEN

After Antony's death, Cleopatra was captured by Octavian's soldiers. She knew she would be taken as a prisoner to Rome. She decided to kill herself instead. Most people say she was bitten by a poisonous snake. Others believe that she drank poison. Either way, it was a sad death for a great and powerful queen. Cleopatra died in 30 BCE.

After Cleopatra

After Cleopatra's death Octavian took over her kingdom. Then he returned to Rome and was crowned the first **emperor** (leader) of the Romans. The ancient kingdom of Egypt had finally come to an end.

A remarkable woman

In an age when women usually stayed at home, Cleopatra was a very strong ruler. She used all her skills to keep Egypt safe and powerful. In the end, she failed to save her kingdom, but her story will never be forgotten.

A lasting story

Today, Cleopatra is remembered in paintings, films, and plays. The most famous story of Cleopatra was written by **William Shakespeare**. His play was called *Antony and Cleopatra*.

We cannot be sure what Cleopatra really looked like, but most people agree that she was very striking. This photo shows a beautiful actress playing Cleopatra. It comes from a film made in 1963.

TIMELINES

Cleopatra's life

80 BCE   Ptolemy XII, Cleopatra's father, becomes king of Egypt

69 BCE   Cleopatra is born

51 BCE   Cleopatra becomes queen of Egypt, aged 18

48 BCE   Julius Caesar arrives in Egypt

47 BCE   Cleopatra gives birth to Caesarion

44 BCE   Death of Julius Caesar

41 BCE   Cleopatra meets Antony in Tarsus

40 BCE   Cleopatra gives birth to twins, a boy and a girl

36 BCE   Cleopatra gives birth to a son

31 BCE   Cleopatra and Antony are defeated at the Battle of Actium

30 BCE   Death of Cleopatra and Antony. The **Romans** take control of Egypt.

27 BCE   Octavian becomes the first Roman **emperor**. He changes his name to Augustus. The Roman **Empire** begins.

World timeline

c. **100** BCE	People in Central America start building cities
63 BCE	The Romans control the Mediterranean Sea and lands in the Middle East
55–54 BCE	Julius Caesar invades Britain, but then withdraws
51 BCE	Julius Caesar gains control of France
30 BCE	Egypt is **conquered**
27 BCE	The Roman Empire begins
CE **43**	The Romans conquer Britain
CE **60**	Boudicca leads a **rebellion** against the Romans in Britain
CE **70–82**	The Colosseum is built in Rome
c. CE **100**	Paper is invented in China

The letters CE are used for all the dates after the Christian religion began. The letter "c." before dates stands for "circa", which means "about".

GLOSSARY

board game game played with pieces on a board

ceremony special actions, words, and music that are performed for an important occasion

chaos being out of control. When everyone shouts and argues, there is chaos.

conquer defeat an enemy and take control of their lands by force

coward someone who is easily scared

despair lose hope completely and feel very sad

emperor ruler of a large collection of lands, known as an empire. The Roman emperor ruled over a huge empire.

empire large collection of lands

eyeliner type of make-up that people use to draw lines around their eyes

fleet group of ships. The Romans used large fleets when they fought battles at sea.

government group of people who rule a country

inherit receive money or land from someone who has just died

luxury expensive things that make life very comfortable

marble hard shiny stone, often used for buildings such as palaces

navy ships and sailors that fight for a country at sea

port town with a harbour. Ships stop in ports to unload goods.

prow sharp end at the front of a ship. Egyptian warships had very long prows.

pyramid ancient Egyptian stone building. The ancient Egyptian pyramids were used as tombs for their kings when they died.

rebellion violent protest against a ruler or a government

respect think highly of someone

Romans powerful race of people that ruled large areas of the world about 2,000 years ago. The Romans had their capital in the city of Rome.

rumour story that is spread about somebody else

sorceress female magician who performs magic by using evil powers

sphinx ancient Egyptian stone figure with a lion's body and a human or animal head

trade business of buying and selling things. The ancient Egyptians became very rich through trade.

violent using physical force. When people are violent, they damage things and hurt people.

William Shakespeare famous English writer who lived from 1564 to 1616. Many of Shakespeare's plays are still popular today.

Want to know more?

Books

Cleopatra: Discover the World of Cleopatra Through the Diary of Her Handmaiden, Nefret, Adele Geras (Kingfisher, 2007)

Famous Lives: Cleopatra, Katie Daynes (Usborne Publishing Ltd, 2004)

You Wouldn't Want to Be Cleopatra!: An Egyptian Ruler You'd Rather Not Be, Jim Pipe and David Antram (Franklin Watts, 2007)

Websites

www.egyptologyonline.com/introduction.htm
A well-illustrated site, covering many different aspects of life in ancient Egypt. Click on Pharaohs and Cleopatra to find a section on Cleopatra.

www.mnsu.edu/emuseum/prehistory/egypt/
A large site on ancient Egypt including sections on daily life, religion, history and art. In the history section you can find a plan of Cleopatra's palace.

www.iwebquest.com/egypt/ancientegypt.htm
A fun site with lots of projects on ancient Egypt.

Places to visit

The British Museum, London, UK
A very large collection of mummies, coffins, and carvings.

The Egyptian Museum, Cairo, Egypt
The best collection in the world of treasures found in ancient Egyptian tombs, including the golden mummies of Tutankhamen.

The Metropolitan Museum, New York, USA
A large collection of ancient Egyptian objects, including carvings, jewellery, and tomb models.

INDEX